Small History

The Shearsman Chapbook Series, 2012

Seren Adams : *Small History*
Kit Fryatt : *Rain Down Can*
Mark Goodwin : *Layers of Un*
Alan Wall : *Raven*
Michael Zand : *The Wire & other poems*

hors de série
Shira Dentz : *Leaf Weather*

Small History

Seren Adams

Shearsman Books

First published in the United Kingdom in 2012 by
Shearsman Books
50 Westons Hill Drive
Emersons Green
Bristol
BS16 7DF

Shearsman Books Ltd Registered Office
30–31 St. James Place, Mangotsfield, Bristol BS16 9JB
(this address not for correspondence)

www.shearsman.com

ISBN 978-1-84861-245-7
First Edition

Acknowledgements
Some of these poems originally appeared in the magazines
Osiris and *Stride*. Thanks to the editors.

Thank you to the Radstock, Midsomer Norton and District Museum
Society and the volunteers at Radstock Museum.

"Since exploration underground is ruled out for the majority due to roof
and shaft collapses, flooding and gas, our appreciation of the enterprise
which shaped the culture of the district has to depend nowadays on
what has been brought to the surface. [...] Radstock Museum [...] holds
custody of artefacts, records and emotions which respect the memory of
those who made, and sometimes endured, their lives here."
—Alan Bentley

CONTENTS

I: *Time Lost*

II: *Working the seam*

"Places are like love affairs. They claim you in different ways. Some live inside you forever, others drift in and out without ever taking root, still others exist in the imagination—in shards and snapshots, slivers of summer light."

— Tishani Doshi, 'Off By Heart'

I

Time Lost

PRELUDE

A pale archipelago of light on the wall, split by dark space, an expanse of shadow. In this gulf, this absence, I trace the lines that remain there, carved deep and ancient now, slow excavation. Shapes that translate into film, and the soil itself, preserved as if paused mid-breath, a mouth opening, preparing to speak.

Stillness is what brings me here. A peace that has forgotten its dark underground, hollowed out by hands, soft strata laced with blood and urine, the sweat of bodies working seams of coal by candlelight. The turning of the wheel, the tramway and railway, a long-term decline.

Stillness is all that remains, since trees grew over the valley. Small traces can be found beneath the new growth still: a piece of rock uprooted from deep below, an enduring metal post, a slip of disused track running nowhere, bare open space where a building once stood, the scattered batches.

This landscape remembers every language, each dialect to have filled its valley. History is what it speaks, its mother tongue. It speaks to you, if you listen, through the quiet and stillness, soft spoken. You can look and miss it all, live within it and not know.

Five Landscapes

I

Marked by collieries and printing factories, a scar, sealed by long grass in wild fields behind the house like thick, new skin. Quiet and overgrown, ageing trees planted less than a century before you were born, or sprung up naturally, somehow, over the shoulder of raw, black heaps of waste coughed out from where a maze of roots now burrows. Batches at Braysdown and Old Mills, heaped tall and solid, like real hills, remind us of a past so different, each dark eye overlooking a town more bloated each year. Hidden now, compressed layers of rock and the thin coal seams, precious work, dangerous and deep below the soft, muddy earth. On the surface, in the light, it crumbles between your fingers, almost oily sediment in the folds of your hands, under your fingernails. Red-brown soil, flattened and creased into imprints of heavy boots, following the same paths worn hard into the ground by a restless tread.

II

I walk out into the garden from the cold of the house, out into the steady, warm light of the late afternoon. The houses and gardens that surround our small patch of land are quiet and still. The far end of the garden, transformed, overgrown with the leaves and dying flowers of earthy potato plants. The pond beyond that. The enclosing walls. There is no-one gardening, getting into or out of their cars, and no distant murmur of a radio beside a lounging body on a garden bench. Everything is still, except me and the soft hum of insects, quivering at the fringes of the longest flowerbed, violet and amber, pale and bright against the left stone wall, just visible within the wet centres of petal clusters.

The daily bloom of sweet pea. Small, tentative raspberries, their blood red juice. The birds, a whole busy family of sparrows, a pair of visiting smart collared-doves, one stout pigeon, call in groups from the leafy branches of the yellow-flowered tree and the holly bush, speaking animated chatters and songs, invisible from their high look-outs.

III

It's across the road, the wilderness of it, past terraces and the dog that barks behind its closed gate. You could walk either way, the edges of the valley connected by their trees, the sloping grassland, the familiar, underlying bed of rock. Behind the house, a route leads through the park, past the neatly trimmed football pitch, the soft rumble of the clubhouse, muffled laughter on Saturday nights. Through the metal kissing gate and over a leaning worn-out wooden stile, you reach the first field. Sloping, a hill furrowed with crests of mud and grass, pitted rabbit holes, wisps of fur and droppings. Down to the line of the old railway, bent into disuse, replaced in parts by a cycle track, thick treacle tarmac, a newer smooth singular line traversed by smaller wheels on the way to Kilmersdon. You come to a long meadow spread flat and treeless, an expanse of grass enclosed by hills with no sign of anything but land or village at its edge, a special site, a church tower on the far side over hedges and meticulously laid roofs. *Jack and Jill went up the hill* here, behind a stand alone house in which a man has lived all his life, the whole of it, with no plans to sell.

IV

Between each point on the map, the brook that can't be moved, that snakes through the valley following its own trail, searching, seeking a wider bed and longing for the sea. Child of a broken river, shattered across Somersetshire, a lost name for where a different boundary line once stood, its water fingers carving a pattern of valleys. Born in its county town, my own course leads to here, where the River Avon meanders into the smaller River Somer with a whisper of origin, *born at the end of the Ice Age*, born of sea miracle and fault lines, archaic. Stretching from its deep, muddy banks beneath the bridge, shallow in wooded silences, off the main road, into the trees. The River Avon, feeding its tributaries. A name that suggests its form, *afon*, chanting river, river past clusters of houses, limestone cities, small, irregular shaped fields.

V

Small roots unearthed by wild noses, glass light, a spectrum of browns and ephemeral shadows, spreading up the contours of the valley in spring. Tales of what men found there, saturated in a lack of light, the damp intestines of the earth, spat out, remnants of a history lost to time. Fossils baked in swamp heat, fault lines that have forged hills, basins, shards of metal rusted into skeletal towers, exiled in wilderness. The earth, locked in sleep but beneath, where the tunnels once were and are now caved in, or empty shafts, split wooden posts rotting in their watery tomb, a blanket of coal dust, a silence that resonates through rock, tree and bone.

Hours

Gaping caverns, circular shafts
would carry them down,
four feet in diameter, though
five by 1800.

Tunnels dark, as if a room unlit
and windowless, the door
locked for hours and hours
and hours and hours

staining skin, coal dust
in your eyes, your mouth,
accentuating each fine line
of your blistered hands

and for some, the guss
and crook, pulling at the
waist, would rub and bleed
wounds washed with urine

until the skin hardened naturally
until the shift was up
until the ceiling came in or
eventually, 1973.

RADSTOCK

"the place is becoming a town"
— *Kelly's Post Office*
Directory of Somersetshire, 1875

I see it, as it is and as it might have been. Stretched between, the gap, the gulf. Change and turmoil, ageing, forming, echoes that resonate in the long aftermath and our own, since coming here, of rooms, places life has been spent. The isolation of the fields, a quieter fear, not knowing codes of remembering who once lived here. I acknowledge a distance felt from somewhere, and walk into it, look into its woods and hollows, trace the outline of its cobwebbed bark. Treading ground long sheltered by the shadow of trees, a twisted veil, elements that make sense, something more than overgrown. A wilderness still more beautiful now than it would have been then, the ground sliced open, carved from inside out, the violence of it, rending the earth. I fill in the space behind and inside, from dust, a need to know, to better understand. In silence as I pass through I picture their faces, the strangers who worked here, there, two places fused into one, their lost time. The market building still stands, the clock the same clock. Radstock, with its short row of modest shops, people in close proximity, not knowing how the other lives.

Home is our house and the surrounding fields. Those that share it could live anywhere, together, and be content. History. Learning to love. Radstock is becoming a town, again.

FIELD, TREE, BROOK

It will all be forgotten later, as everything always is in some way, when life once again assumes its own rhythm. I hold you in my hands, what is left of you now, after so long. You flow from me in uncommon ways, a figment, a vein of silver. I lower you into the water, the small brook that moves through the valley, older than all of us and bloated with memory. You slide into it, almost a glint of scales, a shimmer in the branches of the upside-down trees. The coldness cleanses, a shiver spreads up my arms. My face, reflected, my cold pressed cheeks. I will still see you in that room, that city. In every field, tree, brook. I will see you, but you slip further with the turning of each season, a shadow, still shaped like you but hollow. The resemblance is fading as I walk this land again, the place to which everything returns. Kneeling at the water's seam, I hold you in my hands as you break apart, taken by the current, coursing away in the water's foam. Desire, unbalanced, destroys itself and since I looked, I lost.

TRACES

A fragile mosaic,
soft to touch.
I took my

camera into the
woods again, manifold
variations of lacunae.

Etchings of erosion,
speckled rock, a
chart of greys.

Leafy canopy, blotted
black, white, a
hierarchy of heights,

patterned light through
leaves on leaves,
dappled paper shadows.

Bird droppings, a
stain like paint,
circular, dried up, flaking.

Menagerie of littered
rock, varying sizes,
smaller shrapnel

heaped, dropped, compressed
there might have
been ash then

too, grey flakes,
winged curls, dark
powder snow. This

fabric light, pale
as eroded bone,
head-shaped stones

small excavations as
if someone has
been here, painting,

splattering everything in
explosions of rock
and leaf, fused

in light-sensitive silver.
Dust preserved, a
shadow of itself.

Each scribbled branch,
fossil, tiny circumference
in a palm.

Lines of my
hands, your own
marked by chronicles

our names continue
so many faults
concealed in pits.

Rocks outlive us,
composting trees folding
into damp layers

of leaf. Rusted
oil can debris,
metal welts, an

open wound corroded,
trodden on, crushed.
The peace of trees.

Hawthorn figures in
this shaded place
tumbling into dust.

SMALL HISTORY

"It was all familiar; this turning, that stile, that cut across the fields."
— Virginia Woolf, *To The Lighthouse*

Two hundred and fifty million years, one hundred years, or three. Light brightens through the window as the sun reappears from behind a cluster of cloud, returning warmth to this mild, spring day. We cannot know it as it was then. We can only experience it now, before us, as we walk through it, over it, in it, enclosed by its boundary, the edge of a field, the beginning of a road.

We can dig into the land, with our hands, cut down and plant forests, or a single tree, for whoever is alive to see, but it does not belong. It is ours for the limited time we are here, our small history, staying as we go. The day will continue, the light the same, though the trees a little taller, different birds over someone else's head. Our lives, a seam in history, the precious part we must work, separate from the remaining rock we cannot know and which, for us, is void of light.

This landscape does not remind me of you, it reflects you from my memory. The trees here shadow the fragments of what is still left, in my step, in the grass and the shape of the hills underfoot. Pieces preserved in soft mud, fossilised, cut into deep seams of rock below the surface of the ground, in dark spaces hollowed out and caved in. Invisible traces, too, that we can only feel.

It was in the spring, early morning. Small endings engulfed by rebirth and growth. I left you in your temporary room, in a bed, in the almost light that fell on you in the quiet. The moments then, shadowed by the coming day, the onset of a resumed life after only the briefest of pauses, sit now cast and hardened. A link, a tie, unravelling between us.

I work a different land from you, now, our language lost to history. Our lives, yours of brick and streets of people, mine of a house amongst fields and familiar faces, do not meet. I have learned to live my own way, apart, while you move by the rhythm of another. I only imagine what your years have been. My own, I know too well.

The canary sings. I can almost hear it, as it fades, the almost silence of our small history.

II

Working the seam

COLD, CLEAR SPRING

I have returned. Time can only preserve this state for so long, the shape of what is before me, the gap that indicates what cannot be known. Blossom lights up the May trees, hawthorn or blackthorn, patterns the fields and hedgerows with a dusting of white, painted specks, sharp against the greens and browns of the undergrowth. My dog runs through fields, youth in his heart, as grey hairs climb the backs of his legs and underbelly.

1904

"How little there is on an ordinary map! […] The waving woods, the dells and glades and green banks and smiling fields, the huge boulders, etc. etc., are not on the map, nor to be inferred from the map."
— Henry David Thoreau

The map on our kitchen table shows us how it was, back then. Our own house was most likely owned by the manager of a mine, or perhaps all the mines in the surrounding area. The importance of a person defined then by the number of rooms in the place they lived, how many floors, how many chimneys and therefore, fireplaces. Directly across the valley from our house, halfway up a hill, sit two neat terraced rows of tall, thin, cramped terraced miner's cottages.

My parents sit at the kitchen table, drinking coffee I made for them, small sips. The smell of it in my nostrils, up into my head, circling, a smell I can taste. We share biscuits and the map, passed between us. They trace the track across the two fields and down to the bridge over the river with their hands, pointing, weaving their words as they follow printed landscape, lines of black road across flat, white space.

No sign of the woodpecker that covets its home in the branches of the tallest trees, always hidden, always audible. Or the crowd of wild nettles that springs up in early summer, soft centred almost furry leaves with stinging tips that claw your ankles and grow within days to the height of your head. Small things not visible. Who drew this line?

Tomorrow we will follow the old tramway through the valley's basin and I will take my camera. For now, we sit, the kitchen door propped open, collecting a menagerie of distant sounds in the room that pass in and out, calling to someone, if not to us.

Walking with him

for D

Black and matt, smooth, uprooted from their resting, locked between compacted layers for endless years to be unearthed, speaking what they have known, and laid to waste. We turn them, one by one, their cold, flat, shiny sides above, their dusty, pressed-down sides below, embedded next to each other in the waste heap. We brush off the dust, the smaller stones, caked together in dried mud, searching for an imprint, for the shadow of a leaf or a delicate, winged casting of a life once lived.

The rocks are cool and heavy, a comforting weight in the palm of each hand. They are the waste, the rocks not wanted, lacking the essential compound of coal, carpeting the hillside that would have been grey, barren space, before. Mounds that form waves up high, hidden and surrounded now by a blanket of wooded labyrinth, and the few trees that can grow here, on the waste land, their sparse, new, soft leaves a surprise, filtering the sunlight, shadows falling away to the blackened ground.

In him, I see the young boy, his quiet concern, working his way across the waste heap, hands rooting eagerly for the shape of something on the flat surfaces of these dark jewels, lustre lost in waves of sun and heat. Silent in concentration, he kneels in shorts and a grey t-shirt, his freckled, fair-haired arms smudged with coal dust and minute particles of sweat. Like Braille, his fingers read passages of rock, seeking the bend of a backbone, the splayed skeleton of a ribcage, smaller than his hand.

I find something. A small, broken piece of larger rock holding the raised outline of a portion of fern, the length of your little finger. The sudden urge to leave it where he will find it, so he can show me what he found.

He's going to frame the map and hang it on the wall upstairs.

GARDEN ORCHESTRA

A distant radio sings out its frequency, a woman's high-pitched, falling voice and the knock-tap of a hammer from somewhere over our uneven garden walls. A small dog's yapping bark echoes in some faraway back garden, the ebb of cars and lorries along the main road, a soft and constant stream of engines, birds sing in short bursts and move invisibly in the branches of trees with quick snaps. A bee hums nearer and nearer, the washing machine, in imitation, hums too with every turn, heavy with wet clothes. From inside the open door, something small and metal dropping onto hard, grey slate rings out, in tune with everything.

Park

I

A man sits on the bench across the grass. A leg either side of the seat, he's hunched, head between his arms.

The park at midday. People few, dotted, quiet. A van, a man collecting litter, jacketed, yellow and luminous, mechanical hand on the end of a stick.

A younger man, his son, their dog. It runs, four-legged, panting, towards the hunched over back. He raises his head. *Keep your animal away from me, man.* The owner rushes over, loops a finger in its collar and pulls it away.

A small brown spider, legs in waves, crawls across shadowy white, keeps crawling back.

II

Leaves flattened in one direction, pressed against their branches by a heavy, blowing wind, filtering bright sun.

Where the old playground was, new grass slowly growing from the stretch of mud left after they tore it up. It has grown full and tall, left to recover while the grass around it is trimmed, leaving a circular patch of longer, scruffy turf and bunches of weeds, the occasional dandelion clinging to its seeds.

Lines left from a mower's tracks, staggered pylons on the opposite hillside, the park empty, distilled silence. Not a single person, no cars, the club closed, as leaves brush the seats of the football stand where couples often sit.

III

Trees in the wind, their tentacle branches undulate, swaying like fingers waving, or octopus legs, or hair. The shadow of one like the head of Medusa, huge and writhing. She vanishes when clouds shroud the sun, appears and disappears, a fragile apparition, pulsing on the ground.

Birds encircle your ears, oscillating, chiming notes from invisible heights.

The tree is old, the shadow always new and new again.

A FIELD OF STONES

The keeping of bones in sleep and decay as we pass over them, my father and I, between each deep bed. Calcified curves beneath a deeper dark, the caked clay of mud and a damp that seeps in channels through pockets of air, voids in the earth, along roots below our rooted feet. A pattern of surnames echoes round the stones, a chain of relation and marriage. Only a few have fresh flowers.

1926, a child died. The tiny headstone, blurred by time as if the stone has rubbed away, gives the date, a last name. A violent crack runs through the centre of the rock, the whole thing leaning awkwardly to the side, the age of crumbling. No flowers here, no one left to remember.

We pass over them, lying there, dissembling, careful not to touch them, to damage their delicate rest. Sadness sealed in stone. A soft relief, a letting go. A stress on the moment day is dimmed into dusk, pain inaudible, but there.

I will plant my own tree, in years to come, and perhaps the roots will somehow find me, reaching out their spindly tendrils to my decaying fingers, or the pieces of my hair and nails and eyes, muted to dust, among them. In that touch, somewhere, I will be.

No place for me in this hallowed ground. He wants to be released into the air.

Working the seam

I

Everything we do creates waste. From each seam, body, vein, we seek, extract and place. We select and take. Words cut out and discarded, composting in a heap. Words kept behind, allowed to resonate. Language chosen, selected from the great blank expanse, the sea at the base of everything, a limit that knows its edge.

I walk the lower floor of the museum, past the restored food cart in the entrance, the glass cases that hold pieces of ceramics and handwritten documents, old poster adverts and tools, past the replica of the miner's cottage kitchen and into the model of a mine. Two men, plastic, smeared in dust and smudges of black, shirtless, a rope around their waists, each on their knees behind a barrier as a multitude of simulated background noise streams from hidden speakers. The ceiling here is higher than it would have been then. I can stand here, with room above my head.

A struggle born of darkness, pushed into light, echoes through constellations of remembrance. You separate materials in your hands, like washing and peeling potatoes in the sink, cutting off green sprouting roots, sunken patches of darkened rot.

You grow in isolated places until a small window, a crack in the earth, lets in natural light.

II

Books of scrawls host decades of dust, piled carefully in a box from years past, the inky faces of pages pressed together. An elusive urge, something passed from her to me, written in her diaries, images of us growing, the colour of my hair.

In the museum I read about an accident at Wells Way colliery in 1839. Twelve men and boys, the youngest only twelve, all killed in a cage. The rope snapped, or was cut, as they were lowered into the pit. Their names and ages sit behind the glass, written there, next to helmets similar to those they would have worn, candles like the ones they would have used. Their names and ages are written on stone, too, in a nearby church garden. A shared grave, a mystery unsolved.

I work a different seam from all of them, everyone that worked in those spaces, half their lives played out below ground, work that had to be endured. I think of them all. I think of them surrounded by unnatural night, hope for their hours of clean air, light and love between shifts of darkness as I cling to a place already lost by them, suddenly aware of my years.

A past that haunts, knotted somewhere out of reach. I try to remember how it could have been my father, how circular shafts carried them in a cage, into black clinging air by a rope, descending.

Patio Song

Stuttering bug, tiny and stop-motion, jumps across the hot bricks in the slow rolling of noon into the sleepy hours past one. I sit on the patio, sun warming my arms in their short sleeves, drawing a soft pink line at the edge of cotton, as light pools in each creased palm, pale and shadowed. My bare feet lift from the patio for a moment, cool, and settle again in the heat. The grass sings, the trees. They have been singing all day, filling the space left by the silence of our language. Soon I will begin to think in their song, begin to speak it. It is calming, full of peace and eyelashes.

It is a new song, different from the one I am used to, everything returning to you. Your dark hair against the sheets turns to soil, your body to wood, particles of dust blow from your open mouth like seeds catching the air.

IN THE GARDEN

for M

"I come into the peace of wild things"
— Wendell Berry

A line of trees bend to the wind, blossoms unfold outwards, the coiled promise of spring. Wild flowers in meadows. Conifers, tall and dark, on the hillside. She buys a packet of seeds and sprinkles them by the pond. He uproots a may tree for her in secret and plants it in the garden, wanting to own a piece of spring, its white flowers against the wall.

She gardens in the little time she has set aside for herself. A handful of seeds: potatoes, cabbage, beetroot, sweet pea, their green shoots beginning to climb into the sky. He watches, smiles.

I see her amongst the flowers, the overhanging branches of the tree the birds love, bending to water a plant pot, a seedling. I bring her coffee. *What I think of is the change, the brokenness of it, fractured. Small worlds within a whole.* When I think of her I think of trees.

Night folds itself into evening, stirring blue into gold leaf, caramelising everything until it is sweeter, softer, pulling sleep towards us. In the garden, in the intake of breath before dark, a thousand blossoms illuminate the dusk like a scattering of stars, of seeds, a small hand, cold and pressed tightly in your own.

Two Fields

Soft settling visible light
the point to which we return
restlessly changing, an

unbroken spell, held close,
saturated in the sweet
suggestion of summer.

Such long distances
unspecified locations
but always this

inexhaustible image,
all of us, walking
out across the fields.

Sources

Allard, Bob, *Old Postcard Views of Midsomer Norton and Radstock: Volume 1* (Bath: Bob Allard, [n.d.])

Allard, Bob, *Old Postcard Views of Midsomer Norton and Radstock: Volume 2* (Bath: Bob Allard, [n.d.])

Bonsall, Dr P. M., 'Industrial Decline in The Somerset Coalfield: 1947–1973' (Radstock: Radstock, Midsomer Norton and District Museum Society, 1993)

Collier, Peter, *Collier's Way: History and Walks in the Somerset Coalfield* (Bradford on Avon: Ex Libris Press, 1999 [1985])

Geology and the Somerset Coalfield, ed. by Julie Dexter (Radstock: Radstock, Midsomer Norton and District Museum Society, 2000)

Halse, Roger and Simon Castens, *The Somersetshire Coal Canal: A Pictorial Journey* (Bath: Millstream Books, 2000)

Parfitt, A. J., *My Life as a Somerset Miner* (Radstock: Radstock, Midsomer Norton and District Museum Society, 2005 [1930])